T0072310

BROHE'JE

A NEW RELIGION
FOR A NEW WORLD

MICHAEL EDWARDS

authorHOUSE®

AuthorHouse™ UK
1663 Liberty Drive
Bloomington, IN 47403 USA
www.authorhouse.co.uk
Phone: UK TFN: 0800 0148641 (Toll Free inside the UK)
        UK Local: (02) 0369 56322 (+44 20 3695 6322 from outside the UK)

Published by AuthorHouse 07/12/2023

ISBN: 979-8-8230-8364-5 (sc)
ISBN: 979-8-8230-8363-8 (e)

Library of Congress Control Number: 2023912907

PREFACE

Please understand that this book is a guide to meditation and a reference book to use in the stages of learning meditation, the processes of meditation and fixing yourself. If reading the book in full from start to finish it may not seem to make sense and will only tell you about my story of fixing my own errors and my own accomplishments gained with this amazing skill. If used as a guide to reference back to and use, it will make more sense to the reader as I've tried to make it in sequence and be a handy reference guide (bible :)) of how to progress in meditation and what to do with this new learned skill, the rest is down to you. You may want to challenge my idea's because of the title? but this would be a fool's errand as it's not what it appears and you will look stupid haha! The worst thing you could do is read this book and then just put it down and not practice what I've taught, as many readers do, as they believe they've learnt what this book has to teach simply by reading it. False! This needs to be practiced and if it isn't you wont learn anything apart from my story and gain zero intuition for it. Here's a little about me and how I got here after learning the basics of meditation as I went into seeking knowledge mode to help me find myself on my newly found path. Imagine if some random guy brought up in working class northwest England decided to go to every religion, every philosophy, grift, hustle, cult, intellectual groups, mental health groups, meditators, enlightened people, lectures, quantum mechanics, theoretical physics, the human condition, psychology, philosophy, theology, politics, bulls€$! artists, gaslighting, abuse, memes (loads more) and most of all had fun 😎 And then wrote a book that is only the truth of the best way to enlighten yourself and sort yourself out, with my own ideas of how to do that which don't appear to be being said anywhere else. They worked perfectly for me and I accomplished everything I wanted thoughts wise except for the ego (work in progress, procrastination, way more complex) so the theories were proven from self-experiment and testing! Sounds self aggrandising but this is the only way to sensibly tackle the mental health crisis happening around the world right now as current treatments are failing people left right and centre and these sufferers just end up online 24/7 looking for an answer to their struggle. When I started I was scared of my own thoughts and needed constant distraction to keep my attention away from them. Losing jobs due to always ending in multiple mental breakdowns due to CPTSD, hypersensitivity and hyper vigilance, paranoid psychosis, DID, disorganised thinking, regular disconnects from reality into psychosis, manic depression (literally schizo or worse, but without the voices, well for a month and a bit, but that's another story for another time) and many other issues with a scrambled egg for a brain basically. The side effects of fixing this is building resilience, which also causes a disdain for peoples whine about a single issue or narcissistic cry bully femtards with just depression, so your sympathy is a bit lacking, but so was my social and emotional cues so I built emotional intelligence to counter this before it was even a thing. I'm a polymath and autodidact and wasn't educated by the system so after learning to read and write, the rest is self taught. I have no political leanings, only opinions of the situation and no biases towards anything except I'm a polymath and autodidact and haven't had The thinker for many years, so i don't know what it's like for the average neurotypical or other persons to do what i did? Also I'm definitely not asking or implying for you to do what I did as there's risks and drugs were involved in my techniques and I definitely don't advise, want or wish for you to do that! That's your responsibility and your own choices so don't be suing me for your mistakes made by not listening to me. if you have serious mental health issues? Also I'd advise against learning meditation as it is a risky path when susceptible to delusions etc. as the less stable your mind is, it will have an effect on your truth centre in distinguishing truths, after learning the basics of meditation and needing said truths to progress. Once you take care of The thinker the world is your oyster! Simple issues like overthinking, insomnia due to an active mind, imposter syndrome and the smaller issues affecting neurotypical people, the list goes on and these are a simple fix after getting the basics of meditation and working hard at progressing at it! This is a lone wolf's guide to healing oneself in the easiest and most efficient manner possible, without any bs, grift, hustle or need for "professional" help! Just don't allow your ego to beat you at the first step and make you give up! This is a fight against your own brain and somewhere it doesn't want to go (different if DID) and it will fight you and make you give up early after not even minutes. Meditation is a skill, it takes time and effort to learn this as many Buddhists will tell you. I mastered it many years ago and accomplished amazing things, but i didn't sit there and self proclaim "guru" and start flinging out profundities on social media, as i don't get stuck and neither will you (ooh shiny) Meditation is the key to this process and without it you ain't doing nothing. I will show you the easiest way to learn, as I was taught and then it's a bloody roller coaster! Just The thinker part alone will relieve you of a plethora of issues! That's not even bigging it up as this is egoless, which is another skill you can learn for more freewill, but causes more conscious work in the short term. Anyway you think you have issues and worries? Haha try going my way haha. Anyway enjoy the book and leave your judgment of my grammar, punctuation and spelling as this is my first book and I haven't written for years. Enjoy..!

PART ONE

Free from indoctrination, scripture and control. We will again make bright the light of the angels and saints we have in this world who work in the darkness out of the public eye and bring back the times we held high those who truly deserve it, not false prophets leading you away from freedom and freewill. We are a psychology and meditation based philosophy which incorporates a philosophy brought about by history, wise men of our past, other philosophies, evidence based theories and observations for a life without control with a realisation based journey to enlightenment and self awareness, awareness of others and self control with maximisation of freewill all through sound reasoning and critical thinking away from, spiritual abuse, superstition and ridiculous belief systems based on old stories brought about because of story telling being a great way to pass information on to others in an understandable way.

As we aren't trying to save the world but save ourselves from greed, ego, narcissism, self obsession and the sins in general so we can then in turn clean and heal the world of the wounds we have inflicted on Mother Nature herself through greed, lack of foresight and lack of respect for all living things and most importantly lack of respect for our home! We start from the ground up getting ourselves in order and our house in order with a constant stream of self realisations that bring about confidence in ourselves and our lives which also give us a form of control over the worlds we inhabit.

We believe everyone should be able to live in this world with an open heart, strong empathy, a deeper understanding of others and with us build a resilience to out match any pricks that still walk the streets today allowing us to be ourselves and not constantly having to have a guard up to defend ourselves against those we deem a threat to our wellbeing as this incorporates making wiser decisions about who we trust, get involved with and allow in to our lives and in particular at present who we trust with our money. We don't believe in ist's or ism's or othering as anyone is welcome to join the conversation and turn their lives around for the better and for the betterment of others but without false, tribal, indoctrinated or assimilated belief systems that go counter to our freedom of thought, freedom of speech and maximising of freewill goals and ambitions.

As the wise men/savants in history have come before us and given us their knowledge and wisdom in the hopes of having a better life for you and those around you, but as history shows many have had their work exploited by men and in particular the Romans with Jesus which shows you how common sense ideals and altruistic behaviour and a quest to improve and progress humanity is turned in to a political weapon to control the masses with a plethora of embellishments and nonsensical idealisations of what you should believe, how you should act and who to worship, which don't match the times and didn't even then but knowledge wasn't common place and illiteracy was, so spreading false truths and beliefs was the political norm which today is even worse as it's coming from all angles of society and generally has the effect of making light of the value of simple practices in navigating life's challenges and the goal of finding inner peace along the way as before people didn't even have the basics of logic, reason and critical thinking which was reserved for those only at the top of the social hierarchy. So you had no choice but to believe whereas now you have! We believe the realms of heaven, hell and purgatory are on this very plane of existence and came about by wise men in history who psychologically experienced different states of mind like feeling like you're in hell, heaven or purgatory and personified these in the bible etc, and we can show you this with examples like stating you're dreading something in the future but do you even know what the emotion of dread feels like? and why do you worry about something you have no control over as it's yet to come. The same goes for 'I've been through hell and back' and i feel like I'm in heaven for example, we constantly personify these human emotions and this goes the same for heaven, hell and purgatory, so obviously the goal is heaven and staying there and we truly believe that being in the here and now is a prerequisite to gaining that state of mind.

As with any philosophy there are a few rules to follow that allow these goals to be reached and fulfilled, but they're not as bad as you may think. Like taking seriously the sins as given in the past as they are more important to learn and avoid today than they were in the past. They are much easier to be fulfilled as we are now surrounded by temptation, materialism and are constantly pushed to want them with advertising and celebrities sponsors etc etc. They are the biggest weaknesses that we have which can take over us and make us behave in many ways that lack any sort of respect or class. indecent behaviour becomes commonplace especially towards women and becoming succumbed by desire and or wants is just a bad way to go.

This civilisation is still experiencing a pandemic which has brought about tribalism, death, crippled economies and misfortune to the world and the people within it. we are dealing with something never before experienced in our generations but we also have a front row view of the media, government, political leaders. We can view social media to watch those overtaken with greed and only act in ways as to how best to profit off a pandemic or a proxy war, you'll see all those false prophets created by getting lucky and guessing right in how things are going and what is fact and fiction and the effectiveness of masks (ugh muh freedoms). It will also help you in separating the grifters from the intellectuals and the intellectuals from the jokers in the world. At this point it seems some additions to the sins would be a good idea if your starting a new religion, so let's look at the options. the one's i feel would be useful are psyop's, like the old but still going Russian destroy a country without firing a bullet infiltration of universities in the west and the indoctrination of children ending up with mostly unrealistic wants from the left wing population and having those with crazy beliefs being the face of many major institutions as virtue signalling is the norm now and every Twitter/ Facebook account for high up companies and institutions seems to be run by a Pronoun pronouncing, Trump hating, everyone who disagrees with me is a Nazi type Npc which gives a false perception of how said companies and institutions may actually think or what their possible political leanings are, and with Go Woke, Go Broke seeming to be true.. well let's see. That's actually funny and if this wasn't a book I'd lol but anyway neither i nor we have any political stance so we'll leave it at that.

Getting back to updating the sins, maybe Cryto? as it consumes your whole self, steals your identity, has probably taken hundreds or even thousands of peoples life savings by crypto scammers using your Greed to take it from you which i know because they've tried it on me many times on Facebook, and being the curious cat I am i played along and these guys play a long game, like over a few days building your trust and showing you how to make money instantly and Greed kicks in and poof your moneys gone! They're usually Asian females so look out... I guess it also gives the Chinese hackers something better to do than farm gold in World of Warcraft, Fentanyl abuse no need to explain. Also while talking about the world and thinking of North Korea, don't you think leaders haven't invaded and saved millions from starvation and cruelty in a dystopian dictatorship and just leave it as a kind of backup incase of a major loss of population and then invade and take a bunch of fresh subdued tax payers to fill the gap? sorry my head jumps from topic to topic a lot and I'm fighting it here! Anyway the sins are open to suggestion so feel free to let us know your feelings by the email stated later and I'll pop down the funeral home and get stone tablets and a chisel and get to work.

Allow yourself religious freedom while also having goals and aspirations for understanding that aren't countered by religious beliefs as you can't have beliefs and rules that go counter to the math and scientific truths as this invalidates your religious beliefs and cognitive dissonance kicks in and the mental toll isn't worth it. Take for instance a young earth creationist who drives a car powered by oil and built by metal that can only of come about by the passage of time in the realms of billions of years not a few thousand years which is obvious to anyone who understands how various elements are created by to stars going super nova and how oil is formed from organic material deposited as sediment on the sea bed and broken down over millions of years in to pockets of oil, so in essence you're at least a hypocrite for owning a car or just a flat out liar when it's comes to preaching time as everything you say would just put you in a cognitive dissonance hell hole unless you're just absolutely ignorant of the facts. Like the meat paradox of being an animal lover but also eating meat, as i do genuinely feel bad about how the meat i eat is produced, but i still eat it and have no desire to be a vegetarian as virtue signalling isn't my thing and if someone deems me to be of a lesser moral standing then so be it, I'll just enjoy my meat while they eat rabbit food. Give your brain a rest, get rid of the nonsense and have a fresh start with just a couple of beliefs, and a whole new world is opened up to you with so much knowledge it'll take years to catch up to those unmolested by doctrine and scripture.

Obviously these aren't the words of God nor do i claim them to be, these words are mine and are based around my want to teach others the amazing ability's gained by becoming a competent meditator and what you can achieve by taking some self responsibility and putting the work in to fix what we deem as flaws in the workings of our brains. Metaphorically speaking This civilisations flood is still ongoing and yes it's awful, taken many lives and shown the inadequacies of government's and freedom of travel, but we have to move on and forgive ourselves and each other and progress towards being an enlightened world and work together as we have regressed in some areas and made slight progress in others. I was shown that self responsibility, resilience and the ability to lift one's self from the sins of the world is the way to enlightenment itself and in no way does a higher power intervene In your choices or relieve you of them, if there is a god or gods watching it's a certainty they aren't interventionists as we were told long ago to take responsibility for ourselves, our own actions and choices, telling us we have the freedom of choice to be a good or bad person. It does feel like i was guided down this path and I've no idea what that means, but i decided to follow this path anyway and see where i ended up as it's one of the only times I've felt guided anywhere in my life and actually listened to my inner self because having a bow to no one attitude sort of makes you a lone wolf and this path just felt right..! Anyway back to the book.

Jesus's teachings were sabotaged like some of those before and after and were used by those in power to create a purely misogynistic and warlike belief system to conquer and spread the faith, blended with a heaven and hell style threat or warning to control behaviour, his words were also used for political gain like the romans who did in Jesus's time but were originally spoken as basically just common sense guides to leading a better life and helping those around you build a better life and not allowing the sins and desires to control your behaviour which result in a loss of freewill and corruption of the self which was made very clear that Jesus wanted you to have and maximise freewill and not be corrupted back then as the same as now, because self responsibility and responsibility for one's own actions will lead to enlightenment if steps are taken forwards to reach it when lessons are learned. When self reflection is used and self obsession is reduced, we are then all working towards understanding the self and others better, making forgiveness possible through understanding and stopping self imposed guards and barriers from being implemented to defend yourself against this sometimes cruel world as these barriers stop you from connecting with others with heart, wisdom and understanding. It's not that complicated when you just see a wise man giving some sound advice and wisdom to others because of his advanced knowledge of the human condition and how people work, he would heal the sick easily with therapy and wise words because of his understanding of psychology. Knowledge still remains the greatest power we have and with studying, understanding, empathy and tricks and tools taught to gain control of our minds to bring calmness and self control we become the gods of our own worlds through enlightenment because all these parts we use and open along our path give us permission to gain this level of understanding because we can only be good people to get there unless you're a psychopath but they're not all bad and the world isn't perfect.

The goal wasn't for you to be a sheep in the flock, it was to make self responsible individuals to inhabit and have some power and say over this world, not to be corralled by large governments, institutions like big pharma, secret societies and religious doctrine etc, stopping you from having some control over your own world except for Mother Nature obviously, and transcend and become enlightened and be a god of your own world, your physical space, your consciousness and places you inhabit. Not to idolise the rich or famous or those seen to be above you as they're just false prophets also distracting you from your own self, your own feelings and your rightful place in your world and what it takes to move up in terms of understanding and enlightenment. Distractions are everywhere and temptation is something to be taken very seriously.

The world we inhabit now is at an all time low of individuality, critical thinking, self awareness, self responsibility and with people having no personal goals, no desire to better themselves and just sit on the couch while judging others with a mind incapable of judging their own actions never mind others all the while children are being indoctrinated by their thousands in to states of having complete lack of self awareness, empathy and understanding of others and forgiveness with complete entitlement to what they want and want in the world when they've been confused so badly they can't even identify their own gender. Men and women were created equal but with hijacked philosophies being turned into by men for men scripts and misogyny in the religions, cults and a knowledge and worship of the sun being turned into literal delusion. it's no wonder we have discrimination. Evil things have happened in this world in the name of greed, religious doctrine and war and every time they widened the divide between women, men different colours, creeds and races leaving us where we are now. It's time to put these things aside and stand together as humanity on earth and bloody well grow up and mature and get on with getting yourself in order and our minds in order and then, and only then can you turn to the world and start pointing fingers at what you deem wrong, unfair, unjust, the list is endless but with hope and humility we can tear all these labels down and make change from Truth to power and understanding on a shared level never seen before. It's the best way to make a change for the better without group think or being in a bubble or stuck in a belief system you hold so dear and protect with your life but when asked why you believe those certain things you have no answer which is the most obvious tell that you've been programmed, indoctrinated or forced into a certain way of thinking as a belief should be looked at, critically thought about by yourself and examined in all areas before accepting it as your own and then if asked why you believe such things you have an explanation which is so well thought out, critically understood and explained that people might actually listen and learn, then some changes can be made for the right reasons and in the right direction.

This philosophy will only ask you to have faith in yourself and in big universe terms maybe start with a basic understanding of evolution by natural selection as that's the only real big truth we have apart from actual minor facts about the world but in the scale of big beliefs the rest is mostly theory, superstition and a magicians wand or faith. Like the Big Bang theory etc we can choose to believe it or not but it's a choice from many different theories of how something came from nothing or it's always been there theories. There's nothing wrong with theories as they're usually the best way to finding the truth through experimentation and peer reviewed work which has proved to be the case throughout history and people's imaginations. I've spent a lot of time online and seen so many who are lost and are looking for answers or their tribe etc which i did also at one time but it's wrong, what you should be doing is sorting yourself out first

One goal to set for yourself is to be in the here and now! Now you can look at this many ways but if you think of space time as in saying you're looking at a star 10 thousand light years away it means that it's taken the light from that star 10 thousand years at the speed of light which is very fast to get to your eye. Now you can reduce this to simply being and interacting with others and it will show you that there is a delay of said light reaching your eyes and being processed by your brain so in essence we're always living in the past but it's minimal and doesn't effect us really, now scale that down to your brain and think how much you concern yourself with the future or ruminate over the past, these are both things that take us from the here and now and essentially put you in another space and time to those around you in essence so it's a critical part of the understanding you need to gain and to be aware of to be in the here and now and stay there.

This is where critical thinking comes in handy when approaching a topic someone else is trying to explain to you that you may not understand yet or believe in, but this is the basics and I've explained myself enough to warrant a look at it and take it as a simple belief. Being in the here and now requires a few skills, some understanding, meditation and a want to be there, these said skills are gained using meditation and the rest I've told you and am yet to tell you as we go along. So in the basics of learning and understanding meditation you realise a few things about your brain, you realise you have an inner voice which is you talking in your head and you also have a thinker called The thinker, now when you first meditate and try to concentrate on having no thoughts you'll very quickly see the thinker is constantly trying to pull you back into thought and make you latch on to a chain of thought and follow it. A simple demonstration would be for you to close your eyes, don't use your inner voice and try and focus on a black dot basically infront of your eyes and do only this one thing, very quickly dependant on your brain, passively learned skill etc you will see that thoughts are given to you from out of nowhere which try and distract you from the task of just looking at the black dot. This is what we call the thinker but it's just your mind trying to fight back for control of your brain and make you think, you may very well be addicted to this or already know this etc but this voice needs to be quietened down and maybe eventually removed so you no longer have this in a normal conscious state. Beware any people with mental health issues etc as tinkering with your brain could affect you negatively.

Now this isn't the sole purpose of meditation just to stop thinking, remember this but other uses are for more advanced meditators who understand and know what they're doing, we'll come back to this later. So from your self experiment earlier you can make the realisation that your conscious self is separate from The thinker and maybe have your first realisation? Congratulations! Slow, simple and steady realisations are the way to go as you can do some damage if you're not careful and run before you can walk. There's plenty of guided meditations online and other versions like guided body scans online also, or you may have gone the road of yoga and used conscious breathing to achieve the same goals which is great if you have. I'm sorry to anyone who may be advanced in meditation with my boringly long explanations but we have beginners and novices also to think about, so if you have done the above and successfully completed the goal then congratulations at becoming a beginner in meditation but we have a long way to go yet to achieve being in the here and now. I was recently given an analogy which is great at showing the here and now and this is how it goes, so you lock your dog and wife in the boot of your car and wonder off, 3 hours later you come back and let them out, your dog is so happy to see you and excited as hell because he's in the present moment but the wife hmm not so much…

Now self reflection or just watching your thoughts will give you an indication as to what you're thinking about the most and what's holding you back as like i said there's a few parts to this and your obsession with the future or rumination over the past, or both? may be strong and this is something that needs work and patience to overcome as our brains are wired that way and you're essentially taking the goal of rewriting your own brain into a calmer, deeper self that can stay in the here and now. Now I'm not saying never do it again or completely stop thinking, it's just gaining control and taking the steps forward to a better you that's more in control of your mind and self, then you can make the choice when and where you think about these things and not let them control you, as you will see as i go on and you relate back to the sins from what I'm saying you will see why certain sins control certain thinking and can consume you, like crypto for instance, it's all consuming and becomes part of your personality and the self with most, not all, but the majority, like obsession with money, and basic materialistic desires that constantly run through your mind just make you lose yourself and you become very predictable and obvious to some and in turn freewill is lost, you're easily controlled by others or scammed because you're blinded by greed etc it's just a bad path away from the here and now and this is why said sins exist and why they should be avoided.

Try and see this isn't a Cult of worship or a cult of any kind nor is it really religious in the current way of perceiving religion but more a self religion and philosophy for life with a few beliefs about the world, the mind and those who have come before us to guide us with my own interpretations of who they were and where they wanted to guide us mixed with knowledge from many areas and a mass of life experiences from someone who is humble and genuinely just wants to help people have a better life and lose the self imposed and world made restrictions imposed on us that don't allow progress towards enlightenment, understanding and being who we were meant to be in this short life. I live a humble and simple life, I'm not privileged or rich or have any credentials but i'am a polymath and autodidact with a lot of life experience in the real world and online and have felt guided to this point and now feel it's a good time to share what I've learned along my journey of a modest forty three years, I'm not really saying anything profound, secret or not already trialed in universities. I've been broken and broke myself a few times along the way but I've always put myself back together and grown stronger and more resilient every time and kept going with my meditation and research and kept my fascination with the human condition, psychology and the world but enough about me, let's get back to moving forward and get you moving in the right direction, still without asking anything but consideration of the sins, an open heart and openness to new ideas or ways of thinking and a couple of beliefs.

Now we're done with that, back to the here and now and what it means to you being in the here and now and what makes for a calmer and deeper self with plenty of extra knowledge and wisdom created on the way here. You see this isn't a simple task and takes work and plenty of it but I'm here to make it easier and faster for you while i still literally ask for nothing (except maybe a Mitsubishi Evo from sales of the book) but a listening of the sins and an understanding of how they impact your life and mind in certain ways. Now this is a self help guide and just a guide so i can't do everything for your lazy mind, just kidding, we all get lazy minded and run on autopilot at times because life can sometimes be mundane, a struggle, emotionally exhausting or just unlucky in some ways but still we have to move forward and take others with us if possible into the here and now. Another part we have to look at is ruminating over the past, this could be regret, anger, misfortune etc this is a tricky one as it includes memory attached to emotion maybe strong emotion and some even use the past as a coping mechanism to defend themselves and attack others by way of throwing memories and history at others as a remember when you did this or that or how you made me feel when you did this etc (women mostly) which makes it even harder to let go of and forgive and not forget but move past what's happened and regardless of how brutal it could of been or even mundane you still have to find a way to move past these events and move on as the only thing these memories do is make you feel bad, ruminate, stuck in the past or even totally consumed by it but again this only stops you from progressing and moving forward. I know this is a difficult thing to do and is mostly only completely understood by the religious as they will forgive for murder etc, but this is why the understanding is so important in the goal of knowing thy self and moving forward, I can't tell you to do it and I'm sure you'd even resist your own attempts but this is a must for moving on and is a prerequisite to reaching the here and now. Now looking at the future and being consumed by it, first example being greed and the want for more of whatever it is you greed for wether money or food etc, see i said want not need as a need is different in many ways and could just be a part of the struggle that is life for some for example, but a want is something you shouldn't be allowing to rule your thoughts or time as you could even become delusional about it or on a search for a quick fix or even gamble your way towards your want and we all know the house always wins and then your in debt and looking for money but when you started you already had it. There is no blame here or judgement as that's not fair to anyone and makes you a fool in a bad way as we've all been places we shouldn't and taken unacceptable risk in life's choices and conscious decisions.

The future is unpredictable in most ways and not something we should focus on constantly or allow ourselves to be consumed by it through sin or others ways so this is just advice and a guide to towards reaching the here and now and disregarding those who say it's easy or airy fairy their way around it, it's difficult and also serious in the need for understanding of these certain parts which are prerequisites for reaching the here and now. Now the present, this is easier as it's what we've already processed earlier and pertains to knowing thy self, being self reflective and really getting to know what's going on in your mind, like how loud The thinker is, how you use your inner voice, how you relate to the past and future, quietening The thinker and slowing your mind and finding calm in your mind while observing what's happening around you and really getting a good understanding of what you need to do to find calm and peace wether that be temporary or your skilled enough to have it on a switch. We're all at different levels but time, study and practice will help you get further along the path to being an amateur meditator, moderate meditator or even a pro, but like any skill it takes time and we have to be patient in our efforts and patient with ourselves to retain the knowledge gained and turn it into wisdom and understanding. There so much online that will also help, just stay away from the woo woo and the charlatans who are like cult leaders on Facebook and Twitter for example as they're just grifters using what they know to gain your cash. Meditation isn't supposed to consume your life or become your personality which many people forget and fall into the trap of staying there, when it's just another thing to try and master then move on to the next while holding meditation as a new skill you use when needed or just allow to run in the background as you casually walk around the here and now with a clear mind without noise or disturbance as this is the end goal when mastered.

Along the way you may pick up other philosophies like Buddhism or Taoism but don't allow yourself to become them or let them rule you as like meditation they are something to be learned and understood then on to the next, take the parts that agree with you and move on. Those are two of the most none indoctrinating ones out there by the way and won't leave you feeling you have to follow some strict code or to hell with you type beliefs, they have good advice for maintaining a balanced self but still with freedom of thought, speech and maximisation of freewill, but also contain mythology and i just take what's useful and move on. I'm also showing you and trying to guide you down that path toward the here and now as we move forward and you come more familiar with the here and now you'll realise it's more of a mindset than a belief which will make it easier to understand, process and relate to as it's feeling is very freeing and allows you to see, hear and observe much more of what's happening around you and in your world. Information is much easier to process and many of the parts become an unconscious action and don't need constant thought or concentration as you become comfortable in your new home. Please understand that people with mental health issues can gain a negative state if this is practiced so I don't advise taking this route but it's up to you as your free to choose to take a risk.

At this point I highly suggest you take an MBTI personality test which is free online and delve in to the rabbit hole of looking at how your brain works in a slightly more advanced way, while also finding out more about yourself as you can compare yourself to others MBTI types and also look at the various personality traits that come from your own self and Personality type. Some may see this as a bit of fun, but it's based on Carl Jung's theories and is widely believed by many to be true from the self experiences seen by many. The best example of how this is shown is the way that some people's personalities completely change when they drink certain alcohol or take various drugs. The drinker can be a violent offender while drinking, while also being a nice well rounded person when sober which shows why for some alcohol is very bad instead of just generally bad and also shows how your mind can hold different personas and the shadow self which is also Jung's theories which can be the ugly side of someone who isn't self aware enough to see this change and is a victim of their own mind which leads them to also make more victims because of their switch of personas or being the shadow self and being violent. With these examples i also take Jung's theories seriously but with a pinch of skepticism as it's subject to change from further evidence of other theories and i don't believe all of his work etc but we can only work with what we have and what we can relate too when making evidence based decisions about what we see in others and ourselves when we take the time to properly look and examine our own worlds and others. I've met many with a narcissistic shadow self and most aren't even aware of their actions as they are unconscious actions, but with self obsession comes zero self awareness which seems strange but it's focused on ego and whatever makes them feel better about themselves as the biggest concern is keeping themselves happy which usually ends with abuse towards others which makes them feel better and I'll explain next.

This is usually caused by childhood abuse/trauma which creates coping mechanisms and defences to raise as a defence of ego and self against enemies which can be risen by having a fragile ego due to trauma which causes the shadow self instead of your ego to be your defence against perceived threats and an easily bruised ego makes this a constant want to defend the ego or is raised by being attacked by others which sets in motion this sometimes unconscious action and when you do these actions you're also rewarded because their reward systems get twisted from trauma, so if you're self obsessed which causes zero self awareness you're not going to see these actions in yourself against others. Once you get rewarded for something and you continue you get addicted to that self and said actions as your now ruled by your want for more rewards and change your personality to suit that want! So in essence instead of fixing yourself you cling onto old coping mechanisms which protect your ego from harm but are now way too old and need to be exposed and removed as the removal of these bad parts also allows yourself to make you a better person and allows you to open your heart to others, enabling you to easily show your empathy and understanding of others and self as you progress, as you don't have to be a bad person and maintain this side of you, you need to get it under control and get rid of them and basically stop living a life ruled by your want to protect your ego from harm as that's literally your persona so it makes for an obvious and predictable person in this world which should be full of individuals with freedom of thought, freedom of speech and the maximum amount of freewill you can get in this existence so you can make well thought out ideas and decisions based on good morals and ethics and knowledge or have a shadow constantly pop out, i call them the unknown narcissists as they see few of their own actions and truly believe themselves to be a good person with a splash of virtue signaling to obscure the fact they're a bad person. So learn meditation, know thyself by introspection, self awareness and self reflection and do this regular as it will all come out as unconscious behaviour and it makes for another tool to add to your collection which you don't have to consciously think about as it becomes an automatic process.

Now you're taking on the goal of rewriting your brain to function for what you need or what you want to be in your world and start to gain some control of yourself, your mind and get back the freewill lost due to a lazy brain not taking the time to examine itself, be introspective, self reflect, use self awareness and look at what's going on in your mind and figure out other ways to help yourself progress towards the here and now and become a better person and don't rule out the simple reasoning of simply being an addict to rewards and it's just consumed you. Many people in life are either the abused or the abuser as the abused you can create an addiction between yourself and the abuser especially with empaths as to be an empath you have to have hypersensitivity which is usually caused by childhood trauma and interferes with narcissistic interactions because believe it or not the abused gets rewarded for the act of an attack and they can also get addicted to that persona, and being an empath you can also easily see these traits in others and unconsciously search for another due to addiction to abuse because your reward systems are also twisted from trauma. Some victims are just addicts who need to fix themselves and become a better, wiser, deeper informed person by getting rid of an unconscious want to be rewarded which has consumed you and become your persona and now you're making a conscious decision to either be a good or a bad person and obviously the draw of the addiction is strong as we've always had it but this is willpower and self control to delete that shadow self and take back control of your life and get back your freewill which you lost by allowing your shadow self to run the show in the world and hurt many people who unconsciously give themselves to the abuser and you see this in the abuser unconsciously as it's an unconscious desire for being rewarded and that's why we have so many relationships that go wrong as there's so many types they could go for but unconsciously choose the abuser because of lack of self awareness and knowing thy self and seeing these sides of you. You mostly unconsciously choose the path of the abuser and the abuser gets their fix for the day and unconscious addiction occurs and the cycle continues until you wake up to who you are and what you're doing and maybe listen to your gut for a change and realise how to prevent it from happening again to prevent this cycle of abused and abuser. Raise your consciousness and awareness from the lazy depths of your mind and begin to see who you really are and how you really work and what needs to change in your life and you can make it happen. Learn and use meditation to give you the skills to deep meditation and the conscious rewiring of your mind through a process of forcing the situation in an attempt to make your mind give up on your normal practice and take back your stolen freewill that was taken from you and try and relate to the situation while accepting your loss of the shadow self and being humble and lowering your ego through meditation and accepting the sins as bad, and getting rid of lots of unnecessary parts of your mind which you'll become more and more aware of as we move on towards progressing the self in your world.

So by this time you maybe asking where's the religion, the dogma, is this a version of Gnosticism? No this is a pursuit of self improvement with a devotion towards being a better person, allowing others to be better and hopefully making the world a better place to exist for now, for our future selves and those in the future just by boosting your knowledge of self, self awareness and raising your consciousness to a higher degree. I talk about gods and worlds but I'm only referring to you being a god as by knowing and understanding as much as you can about self and the places you choose to frequent as your world, and gaining the ability to be able to make positive change in said worlds as that's the basics of what a god is, not someone to bow to and worship but to see yourself as a force for change with a humbleness and heart that isn't really recognised today as the old school would class you as a Deity etc. The religion part is what you make of it, it's about what you deem right and wrong and how you feel what lifestyle choices are for the making of a better self and better for all around. Bite size chunks to take on and try and improve on while gaining enough understanding, wisdom and knowledge to be able to predict events because you understand the why's and hows's and making this small part of the world something you're happy with and are happy to be in. It's a lot of work but why not? After learning, act to promote a positive change away from politics and dogma etc in your world and make the changes you want to see not with threat or warning but with empathy, knowledge and wisdom which are lacking today. Just remember i can't tell you everything as this is your journey and this is book is just a guide as I'm not here to write your path.

The old world stories used to pass down knowledge and wisdom of the universe were eventually turned into a religion by the anthropomorphism of various parts of the story into characters throughout history again and again as the character was given or gifted the role of the son of god with a whole bunch of additional belief systems and stories added like class room Chinese whispers added over millennia turning the ancient knowledge in to an entire book and even more books as more of the story is anthropomorphised in to people and places throughout history as the knowledge was way more important back then as now you have a compass on your phone and probably a cosmic guide to the stars in an app, a cat themed paper calendar on the wall and have easy access to fresh knowledge where the boundaries are now in the quantum world with a search for a theory of everything (rules for both the big and small) with imagination, math, experimentation and equations being the theorists tools as they seem pretty happy with the rules of the big as they have a back pocket full of theories like the Big Bang theory to draw from when looking for a theory of everything as sticking on one thing isn't a good idea as they go with the most probable theory at current to explain the universe, it's history and our place in it. String theory is another contender as well as theorising over more dimensions, or the Holographic universe which seems absurd to me but I'll leave that to the math geniuses and those with vivid imaginations who I've looked at and interacted with online and trust me they're as sensitive and reactive to criticism of science and their theories just as much as the religious are over their beliefs.

With a minute to bring in AI and how much of an overestimation of the future it is. If you overlay our universe on the AI's you quickly see what's missing in the picture as we had evolution by natural selection going on in the background within the parameters of the earth, while we with consciousness and the awareness of self were trying to figure out the big stuff and the rules of this universe which is ever changing as we look, as with the AI it just has it's code and algorithms it runs on within the parameters of the program which is generally in a chat program redundant of any use of the senses etc, it's just way way away, ike flying cars and interplanetary space travel, as it Isn't happening for a long time and if it does eventually happen isn't it most likely to come from evolution of the code through natural selection with a question mark over the word "Natural" and evolve in to a better version of a chat bot within the parameter of its chat program, but we're getting way side tracked here, which my mind does a lot but I've kept mostly on point so far as much as I can. Sorry back to stories, so in reality it was just the passing of knowledge of the sun and it's seasons along side the summer and winter solstices and using "the ages" to explain the precession of the equinoxes which has twenty five thousand year cycles which were understood as far back as the Maya and probably earlier civilisations that were lost to climate change or even as far back as the Younger dryas where survivors had no choice but to move and find another tribe to join and blend into or revert back to a nomadic lifestyle while spreading their stories further to the literate and educated people, the knowledge of said equinoxes, solstices, seasons in the northern hemisphere and the the sun and its passage across the twelve signs of the zodiac as the ages! This knowledge has guided ancient mariners by way of the stars for thousands of years and become entire religions with varying beliefs across the world all beginning with a worship of the sun, which was brought about by knowledge of the sun, its yearly cycles and the ages spanning twenty five thousand years. You can see this clearly through history and probably already know this as there's plenty of documentaries etc that explain this in detail about Virgo the virgin and how the sun pauses for three days and is resurrected etc. it's just interesting how a pass down of knowledge can turn into what we see now due to anthropomorphism and story telling as a way of learning. Who knows how far back this knowledge goes as recent discoveries at Gobekli Tepe in Turkey have shown discrepancies in the belief of when humans switched from hunter gatherers to farming and agriculture, domestication of plants and animals, culture and a stability which allowed time for the wealthy and educated to create a system of teaching the illiterate and children to a higher degree allowing them to make observations of the world and the universe they inhabited with reason and logic until it was abandoned for story telling, worship and superstition. In terms of political decisions made in history like Julius Caesar (often copied but never matched) to politicise Christianity and use is it as a way towards a new world order with the ultimate leader (delusion) as most leaders do still try today in the way of globalism vs nationalism and other rhetoric. So I'm lost now but I think we're back to meditating. Before we move on I'll give you my theory haha, I believe that these civilisations in history just had more advanced people join their tribes who taught them farming and agriculture, speech, the written word and for their work were worshiped as literal gods. Just a theory! Anyway on we go.

Yeah so if you become more advanced in meditation by practicing plenty while putting this book down and making your spare time, meditation time.? Then we can tackle the thinker, you know the one sending thoughts to you while you're trying to sleep etc etc. So find your suitable position for meditation which I've found best to be lying down, legs together and straight with the head slightly raised on your pillow. And if you've learnt to dissociate then even better, if not don't worry it's just a bit more difficult, and the thinker you want rid of now as you've now seen it to be separate from your conscious self and just a nuisance in reality, but it's been there a while so it can be difficult letting go of. Ok so get deep into your meditation, like a couple of layers down as your accessing your unconscious mind and dissociating if possible and allowing the thoughts to flow without answering to them or linking onto chains of thought, you can use your inner voice also to say NO (or whatever word you like) when you receive a thought and push it away and rinse and repeat, rinse and repeat, rinse and repeat and you'll soon see it slow down and now responds to your NO by going. All you're doing is getting rid of an addiction to whatever your thinker makes you do, like ruminating etc and with more work and practice will completely shut it down and cure this addiction. Now you might still get things sent to you now and again from various areas but you're mainly now in peace and silence except for your own inner voice. Congratulations as you've achieved something so simple and basic with no risk but what 90% of amateur's get nowhere near after getting bored and ending up saying i don't believe in meditation or something silly. It's a simple bit of rewiring that could change your life if you're an over thinker etc and is usually lowered naturally as you practice regularly as this is forcing it to quieten and speeding up the process of remaining conscious of your mind and observing closely what's going on. Now you can do the same with your ego which sounds more complicated because of its various parts etc but trust me it's not as it's a natural progression with the more meditation you do and the more silence you have, peace and calm the ego lowers allowing a more deeper, wiser and more intuitive self, these things you need to notice as i said you've gotta keep observing the self and i know dissociation makes it easier but it's easy to learn how to do and is just basically another mindset of sorts. When you've got this far and seen these things happening you'll soon see how your consciousness now feels higher as you've taken away a few weights away from it and it's gone up, don't forget if you don't like the feeling, haven't listened to me and mental health problems have shown up you can just stop meditating, stop thinking about it and stop practicing it and you'll go back to your old settings pretty quick, but those of you who are over thinkers who put their heads down on their pillow at night and hear nothing will definitely not wanna leave. So if you've accomplished this? you can slap yourself on the back for your patience, dedication and work as you've shifted a few levels higher towards the here and now and enlightenment. And no it's not another dimension or whatever crap these pseudoscientists, charlatans and grifters have thrown at you for cash! Take stock and remember your goals, being a better person, gaining wisdom, gaining understanding and aiming to master meditation as you devote yourself to meditation as you would do maybe prayer in classical religion. It's really not a big deal and takes little effort in reality.

If you remain still beholden to the sins then it's going to be a longer process for you but don't give up, gain self control and tame these sins like lust (hmm) greed, envy and let them go. Remember you're trying to open up aspects of yourself like humility, humbleness, understanding and replacing those bloody controlling sins i keep talking about because they're usually just dismissed because of religious connotations and bs, but there're purely about psychology, your mind and how to get rid of or control them and stop them controlling you. I often ask why this isn't taught in schools as the basics for understanding the self..?? Or even mindfulness which has made some headway. It's useful if you intend to move over to meditation but if not it's a conscious thing you have to think about and process live, which uses up resources and is just a thinking way of being open to others and not judging. If you carry on with meditation you slowly push most areas unconscious and this leaves you free to meditate while doing things like a crossword etc and I'm not joking. Unless you want to go deep you can run it in the background all the time and just float about in your peace and calmness.

Now from this point we really need some effort, time and patience to really understand meditation and do some study of psychology which is still in many ways theory or evidence by trial and error. Having any serious mental health issues the risks are greater to make yourself worse before you get better as emotions are a no go zone and you could be heavily reliant on coping mechanisms you already have with heavy illnesses like **BPD**, schizophrenia and others. Now in theory a schizophrenic would benefit a lot from this journey but man you're gonna break a few times, get overloaded and maybe even have panic attacks so please think twice before attempting these methods of meditation and practicing it. Narcissist's etc won't matter as they're a simple fix as most are just early years trauma created coping mechanisms so if you're a narc and want to be better and stop being a prick listen up as all you have is a fragile ego and childish coping mechanisms. Your journey is very much the same but you want to study Jung's shadow self and use the same tactic as used earlier by allowing the shadow self out while meditating and in calm and peace (which is your safe space btw I promise) just watch and observe your thoughts and memories with the realisation of them being separate from your conscious self and see the needs of your twisted reward systems, which reward you for being a prick. These thoughts need to be controlled and stopped with the same methods as above and with regular practice of meditation your ego will lower naturally and the ego you fight to defend is no longer your problem so you better find something else to do with your mind and it better be to better yourself and stop being a prick. Now if you're fully fledged NPD..? and want to be a better person..? this is much more difficult as your whole archetype is a narcissist whereas the traits guys just have a few traits in the shadow self as you have the inner child to deal with who's stamped on the shadow so your archetype is narcissistic, your shadow is narcissistic and your inner child is narcissistic pfft I've only run one experiment on this as I'm not a narc and unfortunately the success only came about by letting this person use their NPD on me while i let my archetype The heyoka clown fight back for me and defend me, which it did but wasn't pleasant and this allowed the NPD to see himself in the mirror as vampires don't normally reflect but I'm the Heyoka of our time and can reflect very well (like empaths) so the NPD naturally falls for their own reflection and turn into seduction mode etc and things get serious and very wild, you've just gotta remain dissociated and observe your own actions to realise them in aid of rectifying them as until you truly know thy self, realise thy self and accept your bad actions as your own and repent, you ain't going nowhere.

Now we're even deeper in meditation and more proficient and have at least taken the time to build a place you can go to in your depths of meditation as to have a backup method to the next challenge. Now I'm not advising you, guiding or directing you in this section as there's dangers, symptoms, and irreversible changes being made to your memory. This is tried and tested by me on me and was a success at first attempt and worked but can be seen as "cheating" dangerous and risky and all I'm going to tell you is what i did and you should have now more freewill, renewed confidence and free thinking to make a call on wether you think it's for you or not? but I'll say again to cover my ass that i am in no way telling you to do this. So at this time i was figuring out how to stop emotionally attached memories from arising out of nowhere and spoiling my peace and calm. So i went super deep even with the aid of some indica with high CBD and low THC weed. So after meditating for a while I thought of something funny and went Minority Report style viewing of my traumatic memories and could just pick them up and throw them back which I was super chuffed with accomplishing.

So I thought about it and decided to see if i could pick a traumatic memory and get rid of the emotion attached. So i held the memory up and kept looking at the memory while saying there's no emotion here repeatedly... this didn't work so i switched to my place i made in meditation which happened to be a long long river with a gently sloped grassy strip next to the path alongside the river. Here i made clear my intentions of removing emotion from memories and one by one i dropped the memories into the river and watched them float away and it worked... some had to pass a few times but the job was done yippee and now got rid of the pesky complex PTSD I gained over multiple traumas. For evidence sake, I only needed to do this once and those memories have never come back to haunt me and this was years ago. Now hacking your brain and what to do when you've done it is not going to be title of this book as it was just one thing, and was possible by mastering meditation as the key to entry, and using a place I'd made in meditation to get the results which also comes with risks as you need to be running at 100% and be proficient in meditation to be able to create a stable place in your mind, well depending if you have a visual mind or not. I'm not making light of PTSD here as it's a serious problem, but reality check.. what's the worst that could happen by simply looking at these memories and then deciding to scrub them of this pesky emotion.?

Now my story of defeating psychosis and this a tricky one as it used multiple means, tools and tricks to begin to get rid off, I'd had mine for years and it was like a bubble of brewing thoughts, unfinished thoughts, delusions, disconnections from reality and some just truly bizarre beliefs and wants also. It wasn't a mega issue as it rarely popped up but when it did it seemed too irresistible to not follow and I'd get lost in this sea of delusion, paranoia and just generally bad stuff. So again I'm definitely not telling you to do this as it requires at least the skill of dissociation, mastery of meditation and a real control of the meditative safe space you've created in your mind with no interruptions and just a void of no thought, speech or any imagery. So I'll tell you what i did which is something you definitely shouldn't try as this also involves drugs. Now tools and skills going in we're mastery of meditation, a fully created safe space, the knowledge of extra brain plasticity under the drug MDMA or ecstasy. Now i did my fair share in the late 90's early 2000's when they were good and knew the right people and knew what i was getting which is easier said than done, and had an educated guess as to how much to use, as raving around my bedroom telling the Tv I love it etc isn't going to work. So i used low dose = half a pill a night for four nights. So similar style allowing the psychosis to come in to my thoughts and allow it to overcome me then dissociate to have the full glorious view of what the hell my psychosis consisted of and i was genuinely shocked and amazed of the complete disconnects from reality, bizarre beliefs and sin like wants with a bit of lust and flat out delusional thinking. So after pulling out of meditation as remember you're doing this in your safe space and observing, and I'm like damn I'm like low key mashed in the brain man as it's such a messed up place to experience and made me even more determined to dispose of it, so same again the next night but now I'm saying no and pushing back against the thoughts and images and just shutting them down as they arose and just continued to do so throughout my experience and slowly but surely it lost strength and quietened and by the last night I'd defeated it, couldn't raise it no matter what I thought of or tried to do and that was years ago and it has never once been back since. Yippee another success! Yeah could be luck? but i seemed to be winning the fight for my mind and changed it and rewired it from my own conscious choices and conscious decision to take the leap and made my mind mine and under control apart from a few sensory issues, twisted reward systems i haven't figured out yet and the good old manic depression that crosses my path when it feels like it and to top it off an ego that makes me feel bad if i win something or have a success etc and that's why I've forgotten about it and just left it lowered. I know an ego death is an alleged option, but I'm weary of this "ego death" and believe it's a delusion brought about by temporary dissociation. Psychedelics also come with a high risk of doing more damage than good and who likes the easy way anyway. At the moment I'm going with the flow and know the right time will be highlighted to me. Just as caveat here, I soon realised what psychosis was and how it came about? Well it's basically your day dreamer part of your brain which is naturally able to think outside of the box, disconnected from reality and very broad in its tools of use. After this was achieved, sure enough i was able to daydream again which was amazing as i felt like i was regressing back to a child like mind with the ability to truly daydream without all the psychosis attached. You can take this as fact as it was proven true by my own work.

I wonder if this will be printed as it's a bit beyond talking therapies. Well as you can tell as my journey progressed i picked up many tools and tricks along the way and with every step i felt like i became more whole, wise, Knowledgeable and had unlocked a deeper understanding of everything. I've never self proclaimed guru or got in over my head and continued to live a humble existence in the here and now, and now I'm taking the first steps towards making a change in the world for the better. Could be a flop or a best seller? Who knows… I'm not in it for the money or fame as those went years ago with loss of materialism and a obsession with money I've never really had or allowed wants to bother me as i was awake and aware at a very young age and the human condition and psychology came easy to me thankfully. With the understanding of all that these issues take away freewill, it seems to me a big goal should be not losing said freewill, while some who have said we have no freewill which seems to me a very big scale thing, and this belief was talked about and believed by many strangely but I'm the opposite as I've made my own conscious decisions with great thought and reason and in the process rewired my own brain for what i consciously deem to be better and also allowed myself to become a better person according to my own conscious belief of what it means to be a better person. Looks like loads of freewill to me. Also the No freewill theory is wrong anyway as I've checked and tested for a long time and it's brought about by too much dissociation, a missed piece of the human condition (pre loading) and too many psychedelics.

I stopped explaining myself years ago as none really understood me. So I'll pop some in here, some even called me egotistical but with which I've explained is impossible Some have called me a jack of all trades master of none because I'm a polymath but this simply isn't the case as i have expertise in many areas including psychology and the self -me. I hope i show an advanced knowledge of psychology in my words and a good understanding of myself, while being an autodidact or I may not of been able to help myself without those key elements. While also hoping I've shown truth, understanding and an ability to show myself to others to a level not normally available to those with my illness. I'm sure many already know some or all of these things but you never really see one person giving it you all together in one place and I hope that's what I've been able to accomplish in a way easily understood by all because I'm a polymath and if you don't know a word? Go look it up lazy brain! And remember psychology still very much remains in the field of best guesses and theories as to how personality is formed, how the mind works and what consciousness actually is? The DSM is a work of art for diagnosis but when it comes to treatment the services are lacking. Some have gone to quantum theory to try and understand consciousness better but i think the big rules apply here and the quantum field has just given grifters/charlatans an opportunity to add the interconnectedness of the connectings and connectings of all things with interconnectedness, a few points to grift to use, but without even holding a basic understanding of quantum mechanics. Caveat: There's a big piece of evidence against this whole theoretical physics area which is renormalisation theory... after i found out about this i had to quarantine my knowledge of quantum mechanics as theories based on this theory are very much in question in my eyes, anyway back to the book.

The idea that Aliens in our past maybe giving us a help along the evolutionary path or being the long lost gods of ours in an Ancient Aliens style erm no just no. You're an idiot if you believe any of that nonsense (no offence) I think one of the arguments used is the sudden arrival of a civilisation with instant smiths and the building of massive monuments based around an advanced knowledge of the sky and the sun's cycle as said before but this is easily explained by the arrival of survivors of lost civilisations already having this knowledge and passing it on. A belief of aliens being out there somewhere, well yeah you'd think it would be possible just due to the vastness of the universe and sheer amount of other worlds and the chances of some planets happening to be in the Goldilocks zone there's gotta be a chance but we still don't know how commonly types of life originate in ideal conditions, and it's still possible we're the only life out here, and I'd edge my bets on life being out there somewhere, but space travel at a snails speed and our closest neighbour sun being Proxima Centauri, which is just over 4 light years away travelling at the speed of light which isn't happening in yours or my lifetime or many generations to come with the fastest probe ever made only reaching a mere 0.064%

the speed of light which would take it 6.300 years with a crew of 49 breeding pairs to make the multigenerational journey to Proxima Centauri our closest neighbour, thanks to the work of Frédéric Marin at the University of Strasbourg and Camille Beluffi at the research company Casc4de for the answer. Had to look that one up which i promised my self i wouldn't do for this book but I'll give in for some space knowledge, but anyway we can't reach the speed of light because of reasons unknown to me as i forgot lol. Oh because it would take an infinite amount of energy to reach that speed in a ship and would also stop Time i think..? Anyway on to the next.

So we're now at a point where my continued words will be useless if the hard work hasn't been done on your side and you haven't left the book, practiced and come back to it. So what do i say? Wanna see a polymath write about a field i don't bother with to a high degree? History is my worst so let's try!

The 20th century in brief..!

The Edwardian age! Pro war conservatives and anti war liberals. The fall of the Ching dynasty. British Liberals winning but still help the working class as they never have. Japan beat Russia. A new Russia. The Triple Entente. Austria Hungary and Germany getting squished by the English French and Russians. Rising nationalism. The Serbian assassin and the first world War. 9 million dead. Influenza pandemic numerous dead. Another new Russia, another Russian revolution and bolsheviks taking control. 1922 and Stalin comes in to play! China still a mess, Roaring 20's, new technologies. Turkey becomes a republic. Hitler fails a coup. Wall Street crash. Pushes towards nationalism. Mussolini joins the stage. KMT fails and China heads towards communism. Japan beat China. WW2 begins. 1941 Germany attack Russia oops. Japan attack the USA. Masses of propaganda, Germany surrender 1945. Communism grew by being a reaction to American capitalist greed, beginning with J.D Rockefeller which still was pure greed and exploitation of workers. Europe still being the bane of England in recovery. Western peace and a huge advance in tech and lifespans. Threat of nuclear war. The Cold War. And every war was a proxy war then and there after just like now as nuclear war was avoided. China followed

Lenin Marxism. The Chinese make the most of communism and capitalism. Communism number one enemy. Space race. Apollo mission. The computer age and then the internet!

They say "the people" like the rich and wealthy were affected in all this turmoil, only pandemics level the playing field as it doesn't matter how wealthy or powerful you are as the virus doesn't discriminate unless you were in the uk for a time and it was racist for a week or two apparently, bloody racist viruses hmm it's everywhere, must of been made in a lab of nazi's. Well teaching improved in the world, had more peace and life went on with capitalism as it's guide to being the greediest you could possibly be, the working class still exploited by the wealthy and the new faux middle class exploited by the wealthy and the poor get poorer and the richer get richer IT rules the world a guy called Elon Musk buys Twitter for a measly 44billion, I get harassed by Asian female crypto scammers on Facebook and also some money grabbers showing me how embarrassingly they work men for money and how stupid men can be when they're sent a naughty pic of some random person who clearly isn't them. Was an interesting few weeks and i learned a lot about these people online and played with them, wasted loads of their time while thinking if the crypto/grifter victims actions weren't controlled by greed they wouldn't of got scammed. Then i was bored and then i was guided to write a book out of nowhere.. was i guided, pushed, programmed or just told by a part of my brain..? Who knows?? and here we are now in this paragraph. Well at least you know why i have a few things i expertise in as a historian I am not nor am I a walking thesaurus and would have to constantly look stuff up etc. I like to right straight from the head, no thinking, just flow and write.

Yeah I'm back, so I'm supposed to be brain washing you in to buying into my new religion and then gain millions of followers and take over the world huh! No i just want to share what I've learned and help people work themselves towards being Happier, feeling more Whole, having clarity of mind, peace and calm, an abundance of wisdom, knowledge and understanding and cause a smiley face that lasts after you accomplish the most important goals of your life and become a grounded, and wise good person to fight against all the crap you're sick of seeing in your world and all coming together to make the world a better place. Easy Mode! Just put your kids in the cellar, call in sick to work and off we go. Nah this takes a long time and further guidance will be needed, the acts of building resilience are displayed with great courage and should be accepted as huge achievements in your life. Stripping away old coping mechanisms and parts of yourself you want gone are acts of courage and should be seen as so, but we start with meditation as the skeleton key to open all the doors and i can't impress on you how important it is to take it seriously and practice whenever you get chance and become at least proficient at it.

Dissociative identity disorder sounds harsher than it is but it is a serious mental health issue and usually occurs when put under stress or triggered by something or even just at random in extremes, which is where I'd say definitely see a professional and stay away from self help. You dissociate from your normal persona in to either a different personality, persona, possibly psychosis or something else, I have suffered with this myself but i turned it in to a skill, it's an easy but long fix if your not in the victim mindset or have let it overcome you and become your identity. The easiest method is to learn how to control it and use it on demand using some of the teachings already said and learning meditation as the key to opening the door to fixing it or making it work for you. If you can't control it then you can control where you go when you dissociate by creating a safe space in meditation that you can dissociate too and remove the rest by methods I've already spoken about. In serious meditation one of the goals is to learn how to dissociate so you can sit back and watch your thoughts pass by unaffected by them etc. So with study and practice it should come easy to you to control it or have some form of control over it and then get to work. Removing an entire personality is done in the same way as getting rid of The thinker or psychosis. Get rid of places to go and leave a calm and peaceful void to enter if you do dissociate but if you work really hard at it you can probably just stop it but you can't control others actions so this is where you have to build resilience. Building resilience takes a lot of resources and is tiring so just take breaks by meditating and re balance yourself before dissociating and carry on being super conscious of what's happening to you, what's changing and how your emotions are affected and fully understand the process of building up to or being sent into dissociation and then remain super conscious and see where you've gone. The act of being super conscious will block the action of memory loss of the switch so you can look at where you've gone and understand where you are now as it's different for everyone. Being super conscious is easy if your hyper vigilant but if not it can be gained through meditation but the risk is staying super conscious and not being able to turn it off as you've reached a higher consciousness by accident and you might not want it.? Like I've said before i don't recommend anyone with mental health problems doing what i do or getting deep into meditation, however life is full of risks and good old procrastination is a good excuse, but the want to be a better person and have more control over your life should be instilled in all of us.

I need a word to use to explain how what you need comes about by persistence and practice so I'll use manifest (ugh) so now I'll have to go back through everything and put manifest in… or I could let you do it..? Yeah I'll let you do it. So it's about how to manifest what you need to change in your wiring because it's not really a direct action as it's more like tricking your brain in to learning a new way to work with persistence and practice and well maybe forcing and making some new wiring along the way while picking up some new skills and more freewill. Freewill is mainly lost by allowing beliefs to control you and allowing the sins and a plethora of other things to consume you and take front stage of your identity.

Take an MBTI test to find out more about yourself, it's a bit of fun but can also give you a lot of info about how your brain works and what part does what, I wouldn't say it's purely scientific but it worked for me and might work for you and if you're a sponge there's plenty of rabbit holes from there. Maybe you don't even know if you're an introvert or extrovert which when known can allow you to make changes to make your life better and give you an answer to why you do or feel a certain way. Take an IQ test or an EQ test and see where you are and get a baseline and watch how much you can improve with a bit of work. Emotional intelligence isn't spoken about as much as IQ as it's got bragging rights but it's just as important and you should be able to brag about how emotionally intelligent you are as it's still an intelligence and why would you want to be emotionally dumb? It will become more prevalent in job role requirements and such or maybe already has.?

PART TWO

From here we'll recap with more detail and go a bit deeper into a few parts we have already spoken about and give more guidance. Going back to meditation and how it works. Well we start off by lying down with our head raised, legs together and hands by your sides or on your stomach either way is fine.

Then close your eyes and have your one and only goal as seeing a black dot behind your eyelids, looking straight ahead with eyes closed, not speaking internally and wait for the Thinker to start throwing thoughts at you and try to distract you from your task at looking at the black dot.

The Thinker could have been around for a long time and you are probably addicted to the Thinker being there and see it as part of yourself but as you will already know now, the Thinker is separate from your conscious self and needs to be quietened just by pulling back to the black dot every time you get pulled in to thought.

You have to fight it hard and you may think this tedious or boring but it's essential if you're seeking a calm and peaceful mind. Stopping the Thinker is your first goal of meditation as it allows you to have quiet in your mind and allows you to see what that brings in terms of stopping overthinking, reacting etc.

The constant repetition of finding the black dot, getting pulled in to thought, back to the black dot, getting pulled into thought, rinse, repeat, rinse repeat, will take some time but the act of rejecting the Thinker every time and pulling back to the black dot is actually training your brain to work in another way. This goal can take some time to achieve and many give up before they even start or on the first try but it's an essential part of the process towards unlocking your mind and being able to use your brains plasticity to rewire or create fresh wiring to accomplish goals stated in the book. This isn't woo woo or some trick, it's well documented as real and is used and maybe even used by you without realising it, as it happens so often and could even come about just by listening to some beautiful music you haven't heard before, but then suddenly becomes your new taste as this is a change in your brain. I'm stuck in the old rave days of the late 90's early 2000's as my brain was rewired to enjoy hardcore, trance etc, with the help of MDMA as it helps make the brain pliable.

The typical example of this happening without your knowledge is the building of emotional intelligence. This is a product of evolution right before our eyes as we're replacing the use of primitive emotions to a new model which incorporates thinking and conscious acts mixed with emotions. An example would be someone who meets say a dyslexic person and then their job is to treat this person correctly which will involve understanding someone who's dyslexic. Well two easy things to consciously take into account would be allowing the person to speak, and not interrupting them unless they're hogging the convo! Do this a few times and it would become an unconscious act and you lazy brains can then chill as it's automatic. Same goes for someone autistic, just understand they're brutal honesty, absolute candor and strong interest usually in a single subject. Take these things into account a few times while interacting with someone on the spectrum consciously and there we go = emotional intelligence! Now emotional intelligence goes al lot further than that and is also brought about by finding a balance between emotions and intellect, which brings about more understanding of others and naturally makes you a better person as you'll learn to just treat them normally, which i know is difficult for you normies with your label slapping world, judgment and some bizarre desire to trigger those who are deemed different..? = you're a bad person sooo don't do it. Take others into consideration in your interactions, stop being lazy brained as you can be lazy about it after the fact... as you progress you'll realise what I'm saying and see how actually lazy brained you are.. this takes us to grounding and how your laziness stops you from being grounded.

Grounding work is super basic and simple to do.. like how often do you consciously breathe..? Consciously use your lungs..? Ever?

How much of your actions are just muscle memory learned from repetition..? This also relates to freewill and how much is lost by being lost n autopilot in as many ways possible because of lazy brain. Depending on how you prefer to learn? You could just watch a guided body scan on YouTube and find grounding this way and also helps with shutting down the thinker! One second let's give an example- every time you grab your phone and randomly look at whatever social media you use, watch tv, talk, sleep with the tv on.. all your doing is hiding from the thinker and distracting yourself from the big problem that's going on in your head… this isn't everyone, but it'll be many! Constant disctraction till sleep and then here it comes haha, can't sleep due to an active brain… well you've got loads of stuff to process, questions to answer, things to think about, and perceived insults gained during the day to judge and many others. Well you've stopped your thinker from doing this all day and now it's free if the tv is off and it's dark. All this crap is gone, once the thinker is quietened which also mixes in with grounding yourself and being in the present moment. These things are all blended together to create a much powerful, smarter and conscious human. If you'd like to experiment yourself? Just play around and mess about for instance - breathe in as much as you can and while doing this feel your lungs grow in size, feel it, the blow out all the air in a slow fashion until you literally can't blow anymore.. now i pretty much guarantee you'll cough! Well this is because you aren't using your lungs properly or using their full capacity, especially if you don't exercise to a point of heavy breathing. Practice this until you no longer cough and get it all out haha. Walk around bare foot outside and examine how it feels on your feet, consciously move your arms and legs and just play around with your body and get out of your head a feel more connected to it! There's loads of grift around these areas of grounding like breathe work blah blah blah snore. It's not meditation and is just a temporary distraction from the thinker…. We're not doing that here… the thinker is going. Don't forget, any questions or worries after the thinker is gone.? Just email me as shown below or catch me on Twitter and I'll help no problem.

After you've achieved your goal of quietening the Thinker you will see you have a blank void in your mind where you'll only have your inner voice, and the rest is just silent darkness but a calming and peaceful darkness not some scary horror film type darkness so don't worry! Well if you've taken the time and effort to reach this void then congratulations as very many get nowhere near this far and like I said give up at the start. When you've reached this place and have calm of mind you'll still have to contend with being drawn into thought but you have to keep fighting this, but it will become more sporadic and easier to pull away from as time progresses.

The second goal after reaching this point with a good stability of just you, your consciousness floating around quietly in your void is to make a safe place or create, manifest, whatever terminology you like to use. If you have a visual mind this is easier if not then it's quite difficult and can be patchy like something from Star Trek in the holo deck when it's malfunctioning but don't worry it still works.

If you have a very good memory you can use this place to create a mind palace as you've probably heard of in films like Sherlock etc, and that's there for you to play with but for us with issues it's time to create a self place that you can consistently bring back when needed. You may of seen this in movies where the Buddhist protagonist starts to meditate and goes to the place he manifested in his mind to talk to or get wisdom from his teachers, which isn't actually wrong as I've used meditation many times to get answers which are sometimes just buried in our own minds. Anyway so start simple on your safe place and don't go extravagant as the simpler the better, and it's much easier to re manifest later. This could take sometime or maybe come easy to you lucky ones as it took me a while, as I'm not a visual thinker and think this is why i suck at math or it's good excuse! So keep tinkering and adjusting until you make a space you're happy with that's simple, warm and comfortable like my own which i stated is just a river bank with long green grass, a few trees and obviously the river which is calm at first but if I'm using it turns into rapids.

By this point if you've fully quietened the Thinker and manifested your safe space or place then you've come a long way and should be excited and also proud of what you've accomplished as like i said many give up at the black dot or come out with something like "I don't believe in meditation" which doesn't make sense and shows the lack of understanding as it's a very real thing and done regularly world wide by millions. So anyway the next goal is finding out about dissociation and how to use it in meditation, the act of dissociation enables us to remove ourselves from being the receiver of thoughts etc, which i spoke about before in regards to dissociative identity disorder and saying that this isn't the only goal of meditation. Sometimes we need our minds to let rip as we go through life with no Thinker and maybe not even thoughts of our own or inner speech, we get a build up of thoughts that need to be processed by our mind, which could be questions, somethings that maybe caught our intuitive senses or maybe just an argument with friends or family? This is where dissociating comes in as it allows you to be in a meditative state and allow this build of thoughts etc to let rip and allow them to flow while you remain the observer of this, not a participant as we don't want to be attaching ourselves to any of these thoughts or taking on the emotion of them either.

This is something i struggle to give direct instruction for as i had dissociative identity disorder myself and just used it as a tool in meditation so i didn't have to aim for this goal, but the act of quietening the Thinker and making a safe place will have made you spend a lot of time in your mind and should of given you the ability to achieve this state of mind when required as it's necessary when you keep your mind in a void state. The act of doing this enables you to simply watch thoughts, questions, answers etc all just float by as you casually watch from your meditative state, and while doing so all this information will be used by your unconscious and if worthy of keeping is stored and added to the intuitive, wisdom and knowledge memory banks. The example I'll give for this is that at times you'll respond or react in a way that you don't recognise, say for instance someone is arguing with you and you come out with the strangest of words and wonder where the hell they come from!

So this is sort of the fourth goal in meditation as the realisation of thoughts being separate from our conscious self is first, shutting up the Thinker is second and creating a safe space in your void is third leaving dissociating and mind runs being joint fourth! Being able to dissociate from the state of mind when normally processing info into a state where you just let your own mind do the work for you and you just chill and watch and don't latch on to chains of thought or feeing associated with what's happening. I call this a mind run and usually give my mind a run at least once a week to allow the build up to release as if you don't this will build into a sort of anxious type feeling as it's all dying to come out and be processed by yourself, but like i said it's no longer you, it's your unconscious sorting it all out and getting rid of all the junk. Think of it like how a computer works and how it runs so slow as you have this background process you've never heard of taking up 99% cpu and all your ram memory, so it's making you slow until the process has finished. This is common and is just a build up of thoughts etc that are awaiting processing by you, but once you've got to this stage it's now time to dissociate and let it rip, this can feel strange the first time but also fulfilling once you've finished as it frees up your cpu and memory!

The time this takes to achieve can vary greatly as there's many variables including if you're a hoarder and have lots and lots buried away which you haven't processed in a normal brain state which will make quietening the Thinker harder as it will be full of unprocessed thoughts and feelings but if you do this, work in your void and create a safe space and do a mind run then boom you're in for a surprise of how much crap is going to float past your eyes when you open her up and how much relief you're going to feel when you've completed this goal. This is an essential part of mediation and it's what keeps you running at 100% but like i said you've gotta be separate, don't latch on to any thoughts or feelings that arise and allow them to pass by. So if you've reached this then massive congratulations and a huge pat on the back is in order as you've come a long long way in terms of being a competent meditator and using it to its full advantage. I don't promote meditation apps as they take you in a certain direction but guided meditations are ok as this has to your own journey and consciously thought out and processed by you, not an autopilot who's being told what to do after you reach the void.

Once you've reached this level a whole lot of new things are going to be opened up by you in your mind as you've taken some control back, meaning more freewill and also more depth of character due to being more wiser, more intuitive, more creative, the list goes on and if you reach this point my words will be proven correct! Be warned!! As the way you view the world will change massively and you need to remain grounded as much as possible with maybe the help of listening to music etc as you're getting closer to the here and now and many things invisible to you before will now be obvious also your past, but this is definitely not a time to be beating yourself up about the past as that's been and gone and we don't spend time ruminating over the past as that's the wrong direction, don't get me wrong you can look and see things differently than you used to and make changes etc but you cannot allow this to build anger or resentment and just let it flow through mind runs and leave it be.

This might sound far fetched but i can assure you it's very real and when you've achieved this state many many things will be different about the self and the world you inhabit and can be a bit of a shell shocker! Like i said remain grounded and don't go crazy and just meditate to chill if you get worked up about things because you're going to see people differently and maybe those you love etc and now isn't the time to be making rash decisions etc as you've just opened up the more intuitive, rational, logical person you were meant to be as enlightenment brings this to you and is their to be used.. Do not allow yourself to be consumed by anything that is now obvious to you as being consumed just takes away from all the hard work you've done and the freewill gained on your journey. This could happen possibly prior to this but it's usually here where this happens and the new outlook on life can be overwhelming and like i said, maybe make you focus on the past or others etc but don't let this consume you. Who you were before this point is irrelevant to who've you've become, all sins are forgiven and it's time to move on and forward in your journey but also time to self reflect, which can hurt but it doesn't matter as you've left that person behind and are you are the new and improved version of self.

I have been a teacher before and results vary but the most common denominator is age, as the more baggage you have stored makes for a more rough and sometimes brutal awakening. During our lives we are blinded by many things and we unconsciously do many things which are not of good standing which is hard to take for some and I've seen one of my students suffer from deep depression for a few months because there was so much built up that hadn't been processed it was very difficult for said person to cope. This is why I'm doing a step by step guide to meditation which slow realisations to help in making the journey smoother and hopefully aiding in making yourself stronger and more resilient about what's to come. Regardless of how good and moral you think you are? I can assure you, you'll find many things wrong when you reach this stage which will be an eye opener, but you have to deal with it like a mature adult and understand you were half asleep most of your life and run on autopilot a lot and many unconscious manifestations have occurred which you're not really conscious of, or have flawed reasoning behind them.

This process isn't the same for all as those so many variables it can go many ways but it's all a part of waking up and having true self reflection and true self awareness which brings about awareness of others and will open your eyes to many things but is also dependent on how you lived your life so far and everyone is different. This is usually referred to as the Dark Night of the Soul which i caution you to research as there's loads of false information and can lead you down a rabbit hole which you aren't yet ready for as you don't want to start making beliefs etc, as remember we're starting with Evolution by natural selection and taking seriously the sins and that's it for now, the rest will come in time as you re evaluate the situation, yourself and the world and create a super strong foundation and base to work off! Don't be fooled by false prophets, false idols or ridiculous belief systems that go against who you are and where you're going as your main goal now is to create a super solid foundation and don't go anywhere until you've got it!

That's your fifth goal, to navigate the Dark Night of the Soul and remember it doesn't matter who you were or what's happened in the past as focusing on this only holds you back from progressing to goal 6 which is building your solid foundation and at any point you can reach out to my email which will be at the end of the book and ill respond the best i can to any and all serious questions. It's really important you don't get ahead of yourself at this time and like i keep saying remain grounded, as it's all positives from this point forward in being the new you, better, stronger, faster, intuitive, wise and an all round deeper version of the self with a load of new tools and tricks to navigate your world. The only decision you have to make is wether you're going to be a god of this world or you just want to chill..!

I'm really trying my best to guide you in the best way possible while also leaving you to have your own journey made by your own conscious decisions and ideas. At this point you will see its quite obvious that you have more freedom of thought, speech and more freewill. This can be negated and all given up by simply just going back on autopilot, stopping mediating and returning back to your old self, but are you sure that's who you want to be now? I can guarantee this version of you is a better person and your decisions will be much wiser and well thought out, life will become much easier because of this and being taken advantage of would only possibly come about by a genius narcissist, which i haven't met yet so you should be good! Your emotions are also going to be higher so you need to be not drawn in by false prophets and idols who use your emotion as a tool to control, which sounds silly but trust me you'll soon see, and probably a load of idiots running around who learned NLP and think they're some master manipulator but they're beneath you now so don't worry.

Yeah so much of this journey is up to you and i hope you choose wisely in where you go and what you do after your long reflection of self which like I said is going to be harsh and a more realistic view of who you actually were before reading this book and starting the journey of meditation and you will soon see what i mean about heaven and hell and your past could well be hell depending on what you got up to in your life or it may be quite pleasant and more focused on abuse towards yourself which you can now look at with a more understanding self, working towards forgiveness of self and others which will allow you to progress towards being in the here and now, and once you're there, you definitely won't want to leave! Join us in this place with this book which actually tells you how to get there rather than just saying come to the here and now... it's great! Join us! I'm telling how to get there and stay there, while giving understanding of what you're going to go through getting here and like i said, it depends on what life you've lived so far as those delusions of self we have all drop away and who we really are and are supposed to be, comes to the front and takes charge.

Once you've done all this and gotten on stable ground, seen the real self and have more understanding of self i would definitely recommend looking up your personality Archetype as this will tell you even more about yourself. Some archetypes are unique which repeat through history and some are more generic, which isn't an indicator of being special, it's just makes you more rare if you have an archetype that's reoccurring throughout history. I myself found the Heyoka clown which suited me perfectly and is like my alter ego self and is quite fun to manifest and play around with. There's many archetypes to choose from and like i said it's a good way to find out more about yourself and have a bit of light hearted fun on the journey. In history these archetypes were used in mythology a lot and those lucky enough to match said archetypes were held high in society as they were needed and wanted by people as they were deemed necessary in a population and part of the cycle of life. We never hear of saints, real healers, court jester types anymore as it's a forgotten part of our make up, which is sad really as it's a bit of fun and they're out there.

Having faith is about having faith in yourself to do the right thing, make the right choices, and faith that you can move forward away from your past and aim for your future self who I've said enough times is 100% better than your past self. Maybe you've led the perfect life? Who knows but irregardless of that, if at this point you look back on your life and you truly believe you've done nothing wrong then you need to start again and reevaluate what's going on as we all sin and have always sinned, amongst other things, or maybe you have faith in a higher unknown power that will absolve you of your sins? Well let's give you that's but it doesn't help you forgive yourself for your actions, and this is a prerequisite to getting into the here and now so it's time to choose who to have faith in.

Well I think we're coming to an end here as that's a lot of work to do and could take some time dependant on many factors, especially spare time.

Meditation is the key to unlocking your mind and the world is yours from there, setting goals and completing them is satisfying, becoming a better version of yourself is maturing and growing and becoming smarter, quicker, wiser, faster, more intuitive, deeper and getting rid of all that baggage is truly freeing and you'll only know what it feels like if you achieve it and experience it.

I only ask for two beliefs, one being aware of and avoidant of the sins and taking them seriously and the other is accepting that we're here through the process of evolution through natural selection, that's all. Obviously there are many minor truths and beliefs but if you're building a fresh you? It's better to start from scratch without all the belief systems and baggage and just having faith in yourself and others to put the work in and become a new and improved you in all ways for the better.

So I'm going to leave it here and see what happens? It's my first attempt at writing a book so i hope you maybe learned something new, was reminded of something old, or at the least enjoyed reading my words? There's plenty more fixes and teachings to come if this book goes anywhere and there is a want for more and i never stop working and I'm moving onto the emotions next so that'll be interesting and could lead to more fixes, tried and tested on yours truly for better or for worse. I've have much more to talk about regarding the human condition as I've studying it a while and many more tips, tricks, tools and basic wisdoms for a better life. My strongest mantra is - everything in moderation! And i mean literally everything! Well we'll see how this book goes and see if a second book is worthwhile. I wish you well on your journeys if you do decide to take my teachings and i leave your meditation journey to you, as from the black dot the rest is down to you, and I don't want to influence your journey in anyway way or cause you to believe anything that's not true, add a political slant or make you take a side in any of these cultural/political wars currently going on. Equality of opportunity is great but a want for equality of outcome is a fools errand! Ciao for now.

EPILOGUE

Well I hope by now you've realised what I mean about a new world.? I just mean post covid.

A new religion is just a new philosophy for life and with my teachings in basic meditation and what i exposed myself too, to gain these victories, I'm sure you guys can figure some new stuff out and add it too the philosophy... I want to build a whole community of people who are better, want to be better and mostly be better to others as you have no excuse now as I've told you how to build emotional intelligence.

You could class this as a religion in a none classical sense which is open to new perspectives and tools/tricks to fix the brain which would be classed as an open source religion = Brohe'je.... Hundreds, thousands, maybe millions of people all using these techniques (drug free) with a joint goal of fixing mental health issues and just being better all round. I've hit common issues, but i wish i could work with someone who has BPD and is very aware of their illness, how it works and how it manifests, knowledge of triggers etc because I'm sure we could make some long strides towards improving life for those with BPD. Why the hell not? Well I'll apologise now for my spelling and grammar as I wasn't fully school taught and only took the English language seriously in my late twenties haha and I couldn't afford for the publishers to edit before publishing. I Hope you enjoyed my writing and learned a few things. I'm leaving a donation link in my book, but this is only for animal charities unless you want me to have the donation myself? Note it and I'll listen. I have to repeat myself again for my own sake as I'm not implying, asking or telling anyone to take drugs or do what i did, it's just my story of how I helped myself with the aid of more brain plasticity as big problems require big solutions. Many thanks for purchasing and taking the time to read my book as it's much appreciated. I hope you too can learn real meditation and find whatever it is you're looking for mental health issues or not. I wish you well on your journeys and I feel good knowing you won't have to make the same mistakes as me as i broke myself twice in the years spent accomplishing these goals. Peace and good luck!

Id also like to give a huge thanks to: Pavel Souviron for the amazing heyokaclown art work. You can find his work at: The Art of Pavel Souviron on Facebook.

Email: info@broheje.org
Twitter: @Heyokaclown
Facebook: Michael Edwards
PayPal.Me/Broheje

Printed in the United States
by Baker & Taylor Publisher Services